Hot Springs

of the

Eastern Sierra

by

George Williams III

Tree By The River Publishing
Box 463-H
Bridgeport, CA 93517
(619) 932-7590

Hot Springs of the Eastern Sierra

By George Williams III

Published by:
Tree By The River Publishing
Box 463
Bridgeport, CA 93517

Other non-fiction books by George Williams III:

The Guide To Bodie and Eastern Sierra Historic Sites
Rosa May: The Search For A Mining Camp Legend
The Redlight Ladies Of Virginia City, Nevada
The Murders At Convict Lake
Mark Twain: His Adventures At Aurora and Mono Lake
Mark Twain: His Life In Virginia City, Nevada
Mark Twain: Jackass Hill and The Jumping Frog
On The Road With Mark Twain In California and Nevada
The Songwriter' s Demo Manual and Success Guide

Copyright 1987, 1988 George Williams III

Library of Congress Cataloging in Publication Data

Williams, George, III, 1949-
       Hot springs of the eastern Sierra.
       1. Hot springs—Sierra Nevada Mountains (Calif. and Nev.)—Guide-books. 2. Sierra Nevada Mountains (Calif. and Nev.)—Description and travel—Guide-books.
I.Title.
GB1198.3.S57W55   1987   551.2'3'097944   87-16230
ISBN 0-935174-24-9
ISBN 0-935174-23-0 (pbk.)

Printed in the United States of America

Warning: Disclaimer: The author hereby acknowledges that hot springs can be dangerous and deadly places. The author encourages the reader to take extreme caution before bathing in hot springs. Furthermore, the author does not encourage any person to tresspass on private property where hot springs are located. Persons who wish to use hot springs located on private property, should first ask permission of the owner.

Table of Contents

Maps

Author's Introduction

OK, you hot spring nut you, you're holding the best guide to popular and secret hot springs of the Eastern Sierra region. I hope you appreciate the secret information in this book. Because I'll probably be hanged by the people who frequent these secluded hot springs. To them, these places are their private, great treasures. And now this big mouth is going to tell you how to find them. Just don't tell these people I told you. Can I trust you?

Believe me, this little book will save you lots of trouble. You won't have to waste hours, sometimes days, as I did, foraging around the mountains and hills looking for hot springs mentioned on topo and geothermal maps. I've already done that for you.

I remember one time I was looking for Wilson Hot Spring, in the hills south of Yerington, Nevada. Well, as usual, I got lost, got a flat tire, so we camped that night. The next morning I went looking for Wilson Hot Spring. I finally found it. You know what I found? Four holes in the ground with whisps of steam floating out. Not one drop of water.

Well, you won't have to go through all that trouble because I've done all the leg work for you. Any hot spring worth visiting in the Eastern Sierra region is included here in this book.

You know, the more I think about it, I don't know if I should tell you about all these hot springs. Because these are secret places I love and my family and I have enjoyed. Now that I'm telling you, you'll be there when I want to relax my aching body in the soothing hot water, underneath the blue Sierra sky. You'll be enjoying these secret waters that only a few, resourceful people have discovered. But since you've bought this book, I might as well tell you.

OK let's get serious. The Eastern Sierra is wonderfully blessed with water, water, water. Some of the water bubbles up from deep inside the earth, hot and soothing into hot spring pools. Some of the hot spring pools, naturally, are too hot for any human to enter. So I'll show you which ones are safe. <u>Listen carefully to what I say. And</u>

always, and I mean ALWAYS, test each hot spring before placing your body into the water. DO THIS OR DIE!! I'm very serious about this.

This book covers the hot springs between Owens Lake in the Owens Valley, north along Highway 395 across the Nevada border to Gerlach Hot Springs. Of the hot springs listed in this book, only a few charge fees. Most are fairly easy to reach if you follow my directions. If you're expecting to find a hamburger stand and hotel at these hot springs, forget it. Some of these hot springs are out in the sticks. Only the adventurous get to them and enjoy them. If you're not adventurous, find the nearest jacuzzi. And you usually won't find restrooms at most of these places either. So be prepared for this.

Road directions and maps are included to help you find each hot spring more easily. You won't find road signs to most hot springs so you'll have to trust my directions. I know where these hot springs are and I know how to reach them. You'll have no trouble finding them if you follow my directions.

Now listen, when I show up at these places and you're there, the least you can do is buy me a drink or give me your car or something. Have a good time and send me some money whenever you can. U.S. currency preferred.

Another hot spring nut,

George Williams III
Relaxing somewhere in some hot spring in the Eastern Sierra

Have information about hot springs not included in this book or a question? Write: **George Williams, Box 463, Bridgeport, CA 93517.**

Welcome To My Backyard: Paradise

Let me tell you about one of my favorite places. It's a place I know you'd enjoy. It's not far from you. And it will be worth the trip.

It's here in the Eastern Sierra of California. Some call this place the High Sierra. It's at an elevation of about 6500 feet. It's so high up, the sky above you is a deep, rich blue most of the year. There is no smog here. There are no traffic jams or freeway pileups. And there are no traffic signals to drive you nuts.

This favorite place of mine is about a mile from a major highway but you cannot hear the whisking of the cars or the rush of the diesels on the blacktop. It is quiet and still here. The stillness seeps deep into you and calms you.

The only sounds are those you make, the scuffing and crunch of your shoes as you walk on the dirt road or the cry of the hawk as he circles in the blue sky like a black kite .

It is wide open here. You can see clearly in all directions. To the west across a wide green valley, is the border of the Sierra Nevada mountains, some smooth and green, some rugged peaks sandy colored, some still snow capped in August. On the other side of those mountains is Yosemite National Park. East, north and south of you, are mountains covered by the green pine nut trees and juniper.

Sagebrush grows in the hills and rabbit brush blooms in the late summer. The air smells fresh and clean with the rich aroma from the sagebrush. Below and near you is an inviting, moist green meadow fed by hidden springs where red-winged black birds play and feed.

Out here, in what would seem like the middle of nowhere, is a large pool of warm, green water about the size of swimming pool, like an oasis in the desert. Suddenly it's here, totally unsuspected and out of context.

The pool seems to have been carved out of volcanic rock. Grey rock walls hold in the warm water. The water springs from the bottom of the pool each day as it has for millions of years. You can see bubbles popping up throughout the pool of green water. The bubbles make tiny waves that ripple out in circles toward the edge of the pool.

This inviting pool of warm water has been waiting for you for millions of years. Now it's all yours to enjoy as long as you like. There is no one here to hammer you for a couple of dollars. No crowds of people yapping their heads off and wrecking your peace of mind. It's all yours and it's absolutely free.

You don't usually bathe nude, but heck, there's no one around and the idea surprisingly seems inviting. You pull off your shoes, slide your socks off, then your pants, your shirt, your underwear, and slowly slide into the warm, waters beneath a bright August sun and a blue Sierra sky. As you slide through the warm water, a sudden gush of peace flows into your body.

You flow through the water for the longest time. You feel your body relaxing. You feel the tensions going out of your body. You feel the worries and the cares of day to day living, going far, far away where you wished they'd stay forever.

You see a spidery water bug, with hair-like legs land on the water and do his push-ups. You see a large bumble bee pass over your head and hear his buzzing as he goes by. In the sky your hawk friend has been joined by another. The two wild birds circle in the sky effortlessly.

After a time, you climb out of the pool and lay belly down on the warm rock sides of the pool and close your eyes. You feel the warm sun on your back; you feel absolutely lazy. You're not moving a step further today. So you stay beside the water all afternoon taking turns in the water, and laying in the sun. You camp beside the water and eat beside the water. It just feels so peaceful here. And at night as you lay on your back, you look up into a black sky studded with thousands of silver stars. You haven't seen or noticed a sky like this since you were a kid.

Believe it or not, this peaceful place is real. It's about a mile from where I live. And when I'm finished writing this, I'll get in my pick-up and drive over there, swim and relax and watch my hawk friends in the sky as they look down and watch me.

I wasn't the first to find this place. For millions of years, the Paiute Indians camped here. They bathed, gathered pinenuts, chipped their arrowheads, ate dinner, laughed, played, and made love here. If you're lucky, or just happen to set your eyes on the right piece of ground, you may find an arrowhead or two in the dirt around this pool.

The pool of warm water was a special place for the Paiutes. They believed it was sacred. It's easy to understand why. Here was warm, comforting water bubbling up from deep inside the earth, making a lovely pool like magic. Who would think it was anything but sacred?

I've gotten to know this pool of warm water intimately. I've spent a lot of time here, swimming, relaxing, thinking. I know which end of the pool is shallow, where your feet can touch bottom and where it's safe for a child. I know where the hidden holes in the rock sides are where you can place your foot and raise your body out of the pool. I know when the water will be warm and when it will be cool. And I know when to visit the pool when others will not be here. I thoroughly enjoy this place. It is my friend. Like the Paiutes before me, it gives me temporary peace of mind. And it can do the same for you.

I won't tell you the name of this place right now or where it is. It's somewhere in this book and you will find it if you seek it. When you find it, you will know the place as I have described it.

There are other soothing hot springs in the the Eastern Sierra. I'd like to tell you about them.

Locating Hot Springs

Since most travelers to the Eastern Sierra come from the southern California area, this book lists hot springs as they are approached from the south to the north along US Highway 395. Use the maps included to locate the hot spring of your choice. Some hot springs have individual maps to provide road directions.

Though the Table of Contents lists twenty-nine hot springs, there are actually more than forty included in this book. At some locations you will find more than one hot spring. For instance, at Big Hot near Bridgeport, there are actually six separate pools you can bathe in.

Basic Information Included

For each hot spring I provide location and directions, how secluded each spot is, water temperature when last visited, fee, if any, a photograph of the site and the condition, whether or not a concrete or wooden tub is built and if camping is allowed. I'll also give you my personal opinion of each hot spring. If there is no cement or wooden tub, the sight is listed as primitive. Your feet are going to get a little mucky at places like this so expect it.

Hot Spring Etiquette

Even out in the hills, I have found there is a courtesy code. For instance, if you reach a hot spring and a couple or a family are bathing nude, it is polite to wait for them to finish before entering the hot spring pool. You might even leave for awhile and come back. People appreciate having privacy. You will too.

If there are children in a hot spring, most adults will not bathe nude.

There are some hot springs where clothes are required, like Hot Creek and Keough Hot Spring.

Then there are some hot springs where people ordinarily bathe nude. If you feel uncomfortable about bathing nude with strangers, don't feel obliged. Just because others choose to bathe nude, doesn't mean you have to. If it makes you uncomfortable to bathe with a bathing suit on while others are naked, you can always wait until the nude bathers are finished.

It should go without saying, hot springs should be kept as clean as possible. Don't drop beer tabs into the pools. Pick up your trash when you leave. Do not infect the pool with human waste of any sort. Do not shampoo or use soap in a pool. Instead, bathe outside the pool and rinse off with a bucket of water. Be a good neighbor. Try to leave the hot spring as clean as you found it. Hopefully, you will find the hot spring and the surrounding area clean.

Camping at Hot Springs

You will be able to camp at most hot springs mentioned in this book. Usually there will be no fee. Some of the hot springs are on BLM or Forest land. If camping is not allowed, I will let you know.

Equipment Needed

Well, you don't need much. Have bathing suits if you wish to bathe clothed. Sometimes an old pair of tennis shoes or sandals will protect your feet from sharp rocks or pebbles. A bucket or pan for rinsing off will be helpful. Cold liquid refreshment will make your stay more pleasant. Be sure to bring towels. A rake will come in handy at those mucky hot springs. Lawn or beach chairs are handy. You can take a break from the hot water and sit in a nice chair and soak up the sun. Be careful not to be in the sun too long without a sun screen. Ultraviolet rays are much stronger high in the Sierra. You can burn quite easily and quickly. You might want to wear a dry shirt or blouse while you're out of the pool.

It's a good idea to bring food with you even if you're only going to stay a short time. There won't be stores where you are going. You'll be surprised how hungry you get out in the wide open spaces and clean Sierra air.

If you are going to camp, I suggest you at least have a tent to protect you from bugs that would like to suck your blood. You'll need sleeping bags, pillows, cooking and eating utensils, and a stove to cook on. Don't forget to have fuel for the stove. Oh, and matches and a can opener. What else? Make a written list and check items off as you put them in your vehicle.

When Can Hot Springs Be Reached

Some hot springs at the higher elevations can only be reached in spring, summer and fall. If you are adventurous, others can be reached in winter with 4-wheel drive or by cross country skiing. I'll let you know about winter road conditions.

Caution: Be Careful

Bathing in hot springs can be dangerous—even fatal, if you are not careful. Always, I repeat ALWAYS, test the water before stepping into it. Hot springs can change temperature without notice. After all, the water bubbles up from the earth and Mother Nature is not always consistent. I will tell you about especially dangerous hot springs. You can test the water by very carefully sticking your finger in, or if you have a thermometer, by placing that in the water and checking the temperature.

Be sure to bring lots of liquid refreshment—and I don't mean just alcoholic beverages. Drinking alcohol and bathing in hot water can be lethal—especially for those with heart or respiratory problems.

Experts say bathing in water above 104 degrees farenheit for long periods is not safe.

Pregnant women should be cautioned about bathing in hot springs at all. If you are taking a medication which can make you drowsy you should avoid bathing in hot springs. Falling asleep in a hot spring can be deadly.

If possible, bathe with another person. It is safer in case health problems arise. It's also a good idea, to let others know where you are going and how long you intend to be there.

Be sure to drink lots of liquid while bathing in a hot spring. It is easy to dehydrate because you are unaware how much you are perspiring while in hot water.

It is not a good idea to jump or dive into hot springs because of hidden rocks or shallow water. Older folks should be careful when getting into and out of the water.

Children should not be left by themselves at a hot spring. They should be warned not to jump or dive into the water. Be especially careful with younger children. They should not spend long periods in hot water.

Be careful and be safe. You'll have a better time.

Southern Owens Valley and Saline Valley Hot Springs

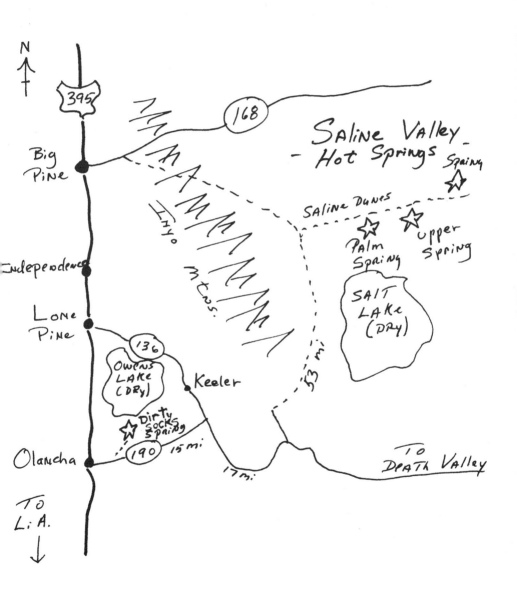

Dirty Socks Hot Spring at the southern edge of dry Owens Lake. Once an Inyo County park, the county let go of the site after repeated vandalism.

Southern and Owens Valley Hot Springs

Dirty Sock Hot Spring

Location: Approximately 134 miles north of Palmdale, California on the south shore of dry Owens Lake in the Owens Valley, near Olancha.

Directions: Take Highway 14 north from Los Angeles to Highway 395 then north to Olancha, a small settlement in the Owens Valley. At Olancha take Highway 190 northeast along the south shore of Owens Lake. This is a two lane desert road which eventually leads to Death Valley. About 4.7 miles out you'll find Dirty Sock Spring on the left, or on the north side of the highway about 1/4 mile off the road. You can drive to the spring easily.

Seclusion: Minimal since it's very near a paved road.

Fee: None

Temperature: 90 degrees farenheit depending on wind and weather.

Condition: Primitive and dirty. A concrete pool about the size of a small swimming pool is filled with sulphorous smelling, dark water. Watch for glass in the water.

16

Camping: Yes, but people may come and go during the night.
George's 2 cents: The pool is unappealing. The water smells and is filled with algae. The climate is hot and dry in the summer. Evenings and mornings are good times to visit during the warmer months. Day visits are best during spring and fall. Weather can be cold in winter. This was originally a Inyo County park. Because of vandalism and misuse, the County eventually let it go.

Furnace Creek Inn

Location: In the heart of Death Valley.
Directions: If approaching from Owens Valley, take Highway 190 east from Olancha and follow it into Death Valley. Trip is about 109 miles.
Seclusion: Furnace Creek Inn is a very popular resort. Clothing is required.
Phone: (619) 786-2345
Temperature: 85 degrees farenheit.
Condition: A plush resort with swimming pool, rooms, restaurant, bar, store, service station, overnight spaces, golf course and lighted tennis courts. Takes most credit cards. A small creek winds its way through a palm tree oasis in this arid, forbidden country. Pool, heated by the water from the hot spring, is open both to the public and registered guests.
Fee: Yes. $2.00 at Ranch but no charge for Inn guests.
Camping: Yes, nearby for RV's.
George's 2 cents: Furnace Creek Inn is a very popular place during the fall and winter. Suggest you make reservations well in advance if you wish to stay at the Inn. A popular event is the Death Valley 49er's Encampment, usually held in November. This consists of an art show, author's breakfast, hikes and more. Call for details. There's much to see in Death Valley including Scotty's Castle, Stove Pipe Wells, sand dunes, museums and more. Furnace Creek Inn is the central point for excursions into other parts of the Valley.

Furnace Creek Ranch in the heart of Death Valley. An amazing stream of warm water emerges from the desert floor and feeds a palm tree oasis. One of the popular spots in Death Valley.

Saline Valley Hot Springs

Location: In the Saline Valley, 87 miles from Olancha, on the east side of the Inyo Mountains.

Directions: From Olancha, take Highway 190, 15 miles to the junction of Cal 136 and 190. Turn right and go 17 miles southeast on Highway 190 until you reach a road sign that says, "Saline Valley." Turn left and follow the Saline Valley Road, 53 miles to the Saline Valley Hot Springs. At the first fork, go right, or northeast. When the road forks again, go to your left, or north down a steep canyon. At the third fork, about 43 miles from Highway 190, there should be a single post with no sign. Turn right, east, and go 10 miles across the Saline Valley Dunes to Palm Hot Spring. Where the road forks, go to your left. You'll come to an area of brush and trees with a single palm tree. This is Palm Spring. Upper Warm Spring is located up the road from Palm Spring about 1 mile. There is another hot spring located farther up this road, about 5 miles, and can only be reached by hiking or 4-wheel drive.

Seclusion: Although these springs are out in the sticks, they are very popular and you will likely find many people on weekends and holidays.

Fee: None.

Temperature: Spring water flows out of the ground at 107 degrees farenheit and is piped to various concrete tubs.

Condition: Excellent and well taken care of. There are several concrete tubs which are scrubbed frequently and bleach is used to keep tubs clean. There are tubs to bathe in and a sink to wash dishes.

Camping: The BLM will allow you to camp here for six months at a time.

George's 2 cents: The first 10 miles of a ragged paved road lead you down a journey to Hell. The moron who named this valley "Saline" should have been shot, or at least seriously maimed. This valley makes Death Valley look like Club Med. This place should have been named Hell, because that's what it looks and feels like.

If you ever wondered where God makes rocks and sand, He makes them in Saline Valley. There are more rocks and sand here than you'd care to see in a lifetime.

Do I sound a little down on the Saline Valley? You bet I am. The road to this place is the most miserable road man or devil ever made. It tore my trailer apart, broke one of the trailer's support springs, tore off the bumper and filled the inside of the trailer with a foot of dust and dirt. I ran out of gas—though I carried plenty— and by the time I got to the hot springs, the transmission lost reverse. Of course, I didn't discover this until I unhitched my trailer. Ever try hitching up a trailer in the sand without reverse?

No, I love Saline Valley. I wanna go back there right now. I enjoy a visit to hell now and again.

Let me tell you about my nightmare to the Saline Valley. It began one early September night around 7 PM. That's when I left Lone Pine alone with my van and a small trailer. I completed the 97 mile trip five hours later at midnight. Everyone I talked to made the drive to the hot springs from the main road sound like a hop, skip and a jump. I was told it was 30 miles from the pavement to the hot springs. It was 53 miles on a dirt road with two signs and no accurate directions to the hot springs.

To begin with, only a fool would visit Saline Valley in summer. Temperatures during the day can reach 110 degrees farenheit easily. Temperatures even at nights are in the nineties. When I left the Saline Valley at 9:30 in the morning the following day, it was already 95 degrees in the shade.

I figured by going out to the hot springs at night, I'd escape the worst of the heat. Well, that was the smartest move I made.

Where the Saline Valley Road strikes off from the Highway 190, ten miles of ragged paved road leads up the desert mountains through Joshua trees. Along the way herds of Jack Rabbits dart right and left across the road. I nailed one or two without meaning to.

I reached the top of the grade and began a long, and what seemed endless descent into Hell, down a rocky, narrow canyon road. The lower I got, the hotter it got. I did not see a soul on this road all the way to the hot springs.

Well, that's not exactly true. Near what I figured was the hot springs, I saw a light in a canyon to the west. I thought the hot springs might be up this canyon. So I turned west and followed the road until I came to a steel gate. I got out to open the gate when a screaming alarm went off and a bright white light flashed in my face. Believe it or not, out here in the middle of hell, someone was trying to live and had erected a sophisticated alarm system.

Two men came to the gate and asked me what I was doing. I told them. They told me it was still another 16 miles to the hot springs. I could have died. I felt like I'd crossed 200 miles of desert. And now

A single palm tree surrounded by a thick growth of brush and shrub marks the site of Palm Spring in the heart of Saline Valley.

A beautifully made concrete tub with piped in hot water at Palm Spring. This and other tubs were made by visitors.

16 miles more to go.

Well, the men invited me in for some coffee and gave me directions to the hot springs. And if these two men hadn't given me directions, I would have wandered out in the desert all night.

After crossing the Saline Valley Dunes on ten miles of the worst washboarded roads I've ever encountered, I finally found Palm Hot Spring around mid-night. There was only another couple out there. Thank God they were there. Because the next morning I roped them into helping me hitch up my trailer. Remember, I had lost my reverse.

Well I've ranted enough about this miserable road. If you can weather the ordeal of getting out to the Saline Valley Hot Springs, once you arrive you will discover a wonderful little camp with more sun and clean hot water than you will ever need.

At Palm Spring, trees and brush give shade to what first appears to be someone's yard. There is a lawn, couch and chairs,

Brush and a parachute shade the central tub at Palm Spring. There is a nice green lawn and a fish pond nearby. The shade is much appreciated beneath a scorching desert sun.

and a tub under a parachute roofed patio. Here there is a place to shower and shave, a place to wash dishes, even a gold fish pond. Though on BLM land, people over the years have taken care to seriously develop the hot springs. Hot water is piped throughout the camp to various pools.

At Upper Warm Spring, a mile up the road, there are two more concrete tubs and drinking water. The hot spring water is odorless and remarkably clean. Five miles farther up the road there is another hot spring which can only be reached by hiking or 4-wheel drive.

One other thing: the place is frequented by people who prefer not wearing clothes. Some long time visitors who prefer clothing, now complain that the springs have been taken over by nudists. So, if you feel uncomfortable in this setting, think twice about making the long trek.

If you like to rough it, you'll like visiting the Saline Valley Hot Springs. Every mile or so along the road in the valley, people leave

This tub is shower for a communal bathing facility.

jugs of water in case you get stranded. Stay on the main County road. Getting off the main road, you may get stuck in the sand. I do not suggest taking a large trailer unless you have a very powerful engine. Hauling it back up the steep canyon could be a problem. Be careful.

Carry plenty of fresh water and food and be certain to tell someone where you are going. It is wise to travel in several vehicles. The trip from Olancha is 87 miles, 53 miles on a dirt road. So beware.

Caution: Desert rain storms can wash out dirt roads easily in this valley. Some roads will be muddy and treacherous after rains. You can get stuck in the mud, and, well, there you are.

There is a way into the Saline Valley from the north from Big Pine across Westgard Pass. (See map.) Many people in cars and trucks prefer this route. It is slightly shorter but rougher. Those with RV's or trailers should come in through the southern route.

Water is piped into this tub for washing dishes. The tubs are neatly separated for bathing, soaking and cleaning dishes and laundry.

This friendly creature and I had a lengthy discussion at Palm Spring about man's purpose on earth. The dog seemed to believe man's purpose was to keep him well fed. Well, I disagreed of course but the conversation was stimulating nonetheless, since he was the only creature awake at the time.

When nature calls, this will be your source of comfort at Palm Sprin in Saline Valley.

Here is another beautifully made pool located at Upper Spring above Palm Spring. There are two concrete pools located here and lots of wide open space.

Upper Spring looking west toward the Inyo Mountains.

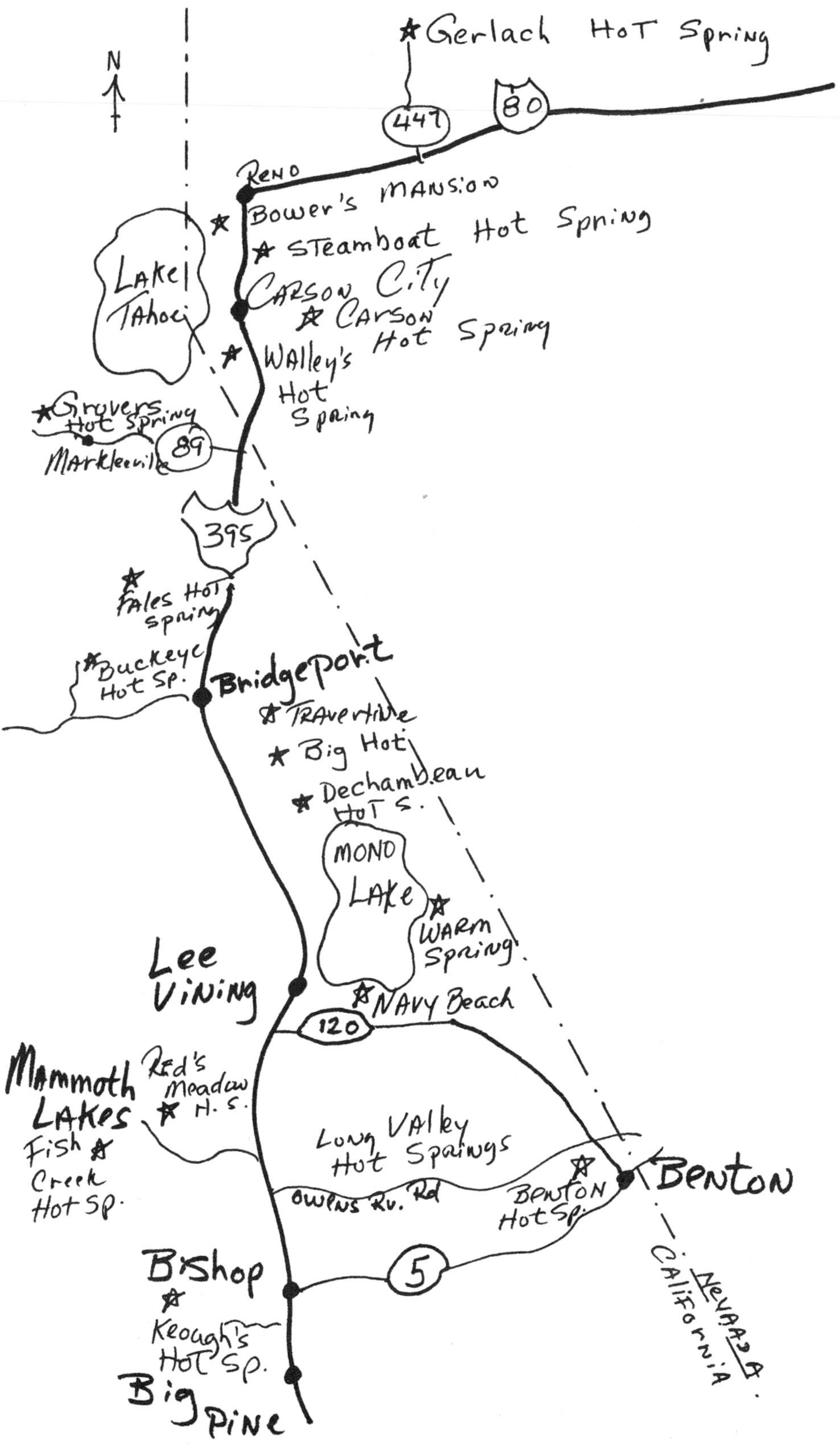
N
Gerlach Hot Spring
447
80
Reno
Bower's Mansion
Steamboat Hot Spring
Lake Tahoe
Carson City
Carson Hot Spring
Walley's Hot Spring
Grovers Hot Spring
Markleeville
89
395
Fales Hot Spring
Buckeye Hot Sp.
Bridgeport
Travertine
Big Hot
Dechambeau Hot S.
Mono Lake
Warm Spring
Lee Vining
Navy Beach
120
Red's Meadow H. S.
Mammoth Lakes
Fish Creek Hot Sp.
Long Valley Hot Springs
Owens Rv. Rd
Benton Hot Sp.
Benton
Nevada
California
5
Bishop
Keough's Hot Sp.
Big Pine

The entrance to Keough Hot Spring between Big Pine and Bishop.

Keough Hot Spring

Location: Half way between Big Pine and Bishop, about 8 miles north of Big Pine.

Directions: Stay on Highway 395 past Big Pine. A road sign 8 miles north of Big Pine points west to Keough Hot Spring. Take Keough Hot Spring Road 1/2 mile west.

Seclusion: Keough is a public facility. You are required to wear clothing.

Temperature: The swimming pool is kept between 87-95 degrees farenheit.

Condition: Keough Hot Spring is a commercial business. A large pool has been built. Restrooms and changing rooms are available.

Fee: Yes.

Camping: No tent camping. Partial RV hookups.

George's 2 cents: Keough's is a nice place to visit if you enjoy

28

being around a lot of people and if you prefer a concrete pool to a primitive hot spring. I prefer to go into the pools located below the hot springs. There is no charge here. The hot water that feeds Keoughs', winds down the hill to these pool.

Keough Hot Spring Ditch offers clean, hot water with pools of varying temperatures.

Keough Hot Spring Ditch

Location: Just below Keough Hot Spring on a dirt road.

Directions: Approaching from the south, turn left onto Keough Hot Spring road, then turn right on a dirt road just before Keough's Hot Spring resort. Go 1/4 mile.

Seclusion: This place is highly visited.

Temperature: Around 95 degrees farenheit depending on wind and weather.

Condition: Rock dams hold in the hot water and make pools with sand bottoms.

Fee: No.

Camping: Tent camping is out, but you might want to sleep in your van or RV.

George's 2 cents: Keough's Ditch is free and it's just off the highway. It's a nice place to stop on a long trip through Owens Valley.

Long Valley Hot Springs

The Long Valley hot springs are a group of hot springs located in the Crowley Lake area near Mammoth Lakes. The locations of the hot springs are mostly known only to locals. Therefore, fewer people visit. There are times during the day when you can visit these and have them all to yourself. However, weekends tend to get crowded.

Whitmore Hot Spring

Location: One mile east of Highway 395 at a point 9 miles south of Mammoth Lakes.

Directions: Take Highway 395 from Bishop north toward Mammoth Lakes. About 31 miles from Bishop you'll see a small green church on your right and a road sign, "Whitmore." This is Owens River Road. Turn right here, east, and go one mile to Whitmore Hot Spring. A swimming pool heated by water pumped from a well is

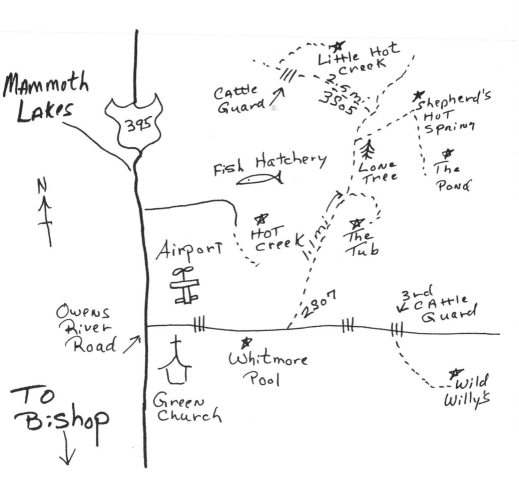

located in a building on your right.

Seclusion: This is a public swimming pool. Clothing required.

Fee: Yes.

Open: All year.

Temperature: Usually around 82 degrees farenheit.

Condition: This is a concrete pool. Restrooms are available.

Camping: Not at the hot spring but there is plenty of lands nearby where you can camp. Owens River is only 4 miles east of here. Benton Crossing is a popular place to fish and camp.

Whitmore pool near Mammoth Lakes is fed by a warm spring. Temperature is kept at around 82 degrees farenheit. Open all year. There is a fee.

George's 2 cents: I do not bathe here. It's a public place although it
is not highly visited. Plus, there is a fee. However, there is a jacuzzi
size tub at the southeast corner behind the pool. This is where water
from the pool flows out in a narrow stream. The stream is shallow
enough for kids to enjoy. There are other hot springs in the nearby
area more secluded where there is no fee. I'll tell you about them in
a bit.

Hot Creek

Location: About 8 miles east of Mammoth Lakes near the airport.
Directions: Just north of the Mammoth Lakes airport on Highway
395, a paved road leads east to the Hot Creek Fish Hatchery. Follow
this paved road and then turn right, or south, and follow the road
behind the airport. You'll come to a dirt road that goes southeast to

A jacuzzi size warm pool is located at the southeast corner of Whitmore pool.

Hot Creek. Turn left at the dirt road and follow it two miles. You'll come to a parking lot where other cars are parked.

Seclusion: This is a popular public place operated by the Forest Service. Clothing is required.

Fee: No.

Accessibility: May be closed in winter.

Open: From sunrise until sunset.

Temperature: Varies from hot to cold depending upon what part of the creek you're in.

Restrooms: Yes.

Condition: Hot Creek is a "hot creek." Nice, but highly visited.

Camping: No.

George's 2 cents: Hot Creek is one of the most popular places to visit in the Mammoth Lakes area. Many tourists visit. It's one of the places I take my friends who haven't visited the Eastern Sierra. It's

Hot Creek near Mammoth Lakes is a popular attraction. Restrooms are available. A park ranger watches over the facility. Open all year from sunrise to sunset.

a nice recreation spot if you have a family, easy to reach and fun if you like a small crowd. A ranger watches over the facility to protect and help the public. Hot Creek can be dangerous—even deadly. A number of people have been killed there in the last decade. The deaths occurred when people strayed down the creek into the boiling hot water and were scalded to death. But if you stay in the general bathing area, you should be OK. Even here though, there are hot spots. Be careful.

Little Hot Creek

Location: In Long Valley about 1 mile north of Hot Creek.
Directions: At the green church on Highway 395 mentioned above, take Owens River road 1.2 miles until you come to a dirt road on your left, which should be posted 2S07. Turn left and follow this until you come to another dirt road on your left marked 3S05. A sign

Dangers of Hot Creek

12 people have lost their lives in Hot Creek since 1968. Many more have been seriously injured.

Some of the hazards are:

**Scalding Water
Broken Glass
Arsenic in the Water
Sporadic High Pollution
Sudden Temperature Changes
Unpredictable Eruptions
Unstable Ground**

It is recommended that you remain on paved and wood paths and do not enter the water. Some of the more dangerous areas are fenced; however new hazards are a constant threat—please use extreme caution.

The dangers at Hot Creek are real as this warning sign attests. The Forest Service encourages extreme caution while bathing at Hot Creek.

should say this is the way to "Antelope Valley." Take this road 2.5 miles to the second cattle guard. Here, turn right and go 1 mile down a winding dirt road to Little Hot Creek Springs.

Seclusion: I've never seen anyone there when I've visited.

Accessibility: May be impossible to reach in winter even with 4-wheel drive. Cross country skiing may be the answer.

Fee: None.

Temperature: Let's put it this way: the source is boiling water.

Condition: A group of hot springs pour a hefty stream of water into a creek. There are several dams where pools are located. The farther you go down stream, the cooler the pools are. The bottom of the creek can be a bit mucky. Good suggestion is to bring a garden rake to rake out some of the green goo that grows here.

Camping: Yes.

George's 2 cents: Little Hot Creek is a terrific gem waiting to be discovered. It's secluded and most people don't know about it. But

The cloud of steam pictured here is floating up from a boiling pool of hot, sulphorous water at Hot Creek. Dangerous portions of the creek are fenced off. In spite of this, people have been killed when they have not used caution.

please be aware: the source of this creek is scalding, dangerous water. The Forest Service has fenced this section off. Children should not be allowed by themselves near the source. Go down stream and be safe.

Wild Willy's Hot Spring

Location: In Long Valley on a dirt road north of Crowley Lake.
Directions: Take Highway 395 from Bishop north toward Mammoth Lakes. At Owens River Road (that's where that green church is on your right) turn right. Go 3 miles past Whitmore Hot Springs. Look for cattle guards. These are steel grates that cut across the road and make a hell of a racket when you pass over them in your vehicle. Exactly at the third cattle guard, there is a dirt road that goes to your

A mist of water vapor rises from Little Hot Creek on a cold spring morning.

right, or toward the south. Take this road and follow it 1/2 mile. You'll come to a dry, white alkali lake bed on your right. It may get a little mucky here in the spring or after a good rain. Ease your way through here and go about another 1/4 mile. Here the road turns to the left and down a small hill. Wild Willy's is located here.

Seclusion: Best times for private bathing are in the early morning and around 4-5 PM in the summer. Fewer people in the fall and winter. Weekends tend to be busy.

Accessibility: You'll need 4-wheel drive in winter.

Temperature: About 95 degrees farenheit.

Condition: Good. There are two man made tubs. A large concrete pool was made by locals. This pool is about 12 feet by 8. There are even concrete benches where you can sit and a wooden deck for

The author rests his heels in the wooden tub at Wild Willy's hot spring in Long Valley.

sun bathing. The water is about knee deep. The floor of the pool is sand and pebbles. Another wooden tub is located nearby. Last summer a Dutch visitor and I cleaned all the crud out of the small wooden tub. It's a two person tub, hotter, and less used than the larger pool.

Camping: You bet.

Fee: None

George's 2 cents: This is one of our family's favorite hot springs. Our children— mine are now 6 and 7— can play in the water by themselves and we can easily keep our eyes on them. They are told not to jump or dive in the shallow water. You can camp safely here and often bathe in seclusion. Weekends tend to draw more visitors. Many visitors prefer to bathe nude.

The large cement pool at Wild Willy's was made by industrious locals. The pool can be drained and cleaned. The bottom consists of sand and pebbles. Someone recently built a sun deck. Wild Willy's is a popular place for locals and visitors.

The Tub Hot Spring

Location: In Long Valley about 1/2 mile north of Owens River Road not far from Wild Willy's.

Directions: Again, if you are approaching from Bishop or Mammoth, take Owens River Road about 9 miles south of Mammoth. Go 1.2 miles until you come to a dirt road on your left. It should be marked with a sign "2S07." Turn left onto the dirt road. Follow it for a 1.1 mile. You will come to a dirt road on your right. Turn right. Follow it 1/4 mile until you come to a road on your right. Turn right and go 200 yards to the hot spring.

Seclusion: This hot spring is less visited than Wild Willy's but it is still popular with locals and others. A good time for private bathing is in the early morning before 10 AM and around 5 in the afternoon.

The Tub hot spring in Long Valley is wonderfully intimate. Sheltered by rocks on two sides, those who prefer privacy will find this one attractive. This is another tub built by industrious locals.

Accessibility: You will need 4-wheel drive in winter when there is snow.

Fee: No.

Temperature: The water flows out of the ground at 114 degrees farenheit. You can regulate the water flow into the tub, and therefore the temperature.

Condition: Good. A concrete tub about the size of a jacuzzi is fed by a hose attached to the hot water source about 100 yards away. Occassionally needs cleaning out. This is done by removing the PVC pipe and allowing the water to drain. Then scrub the tub clean with a brush and bleach. Then put the PVC pipe back in and let the tub fill up. Takes about 2 hours to fill.

Camping: You bet.

George's 2 cents: This is my second favorite hot spring in Long Valley. This tub is smaller than Wild Willy's and more intimate. Some folks bathe here in the evening, camp at night, and bathe again in the morning before hitting the road. I've camped here often with my family. By the way, if you have an AC/DC TV, you can pick up the networks by using UHF. There's a translator on one of the mountains to the east.

Shepherd's Hot Spring (Lone Tree)

Location: In Long Valley about 1 mile north of The Tub.
Directions: Take Owens River Road 1.2 miles to the first dirt road on your left, 2S07. Take this road 1.9 miles until you see a lone tree on your right. Turn right onto the dirt road just before the tree. Follow it for a 1/2 mile. Where the road forks, go left. You will come to a little valley where there is a pond. The hot spring is this side of the pond.
Accessibility: You'll need 4-wheel drive in winter when it snows.

It's been said that shepherds built this tub in Long Valley. Hence the name, Shepherd's Hot Spring.

Seclusion: Visited far less than the other Long Valley hot springs.
Fee: No.
Temperature: Water flows from a small pond at 113 degrees farenheit. You can cool the tub by diverting the hot water.
Condition: Good. This is a small man made concrete tub. Four can get in comfortably.
Camping: Yes and you will be less disturbed because fewer people know about this hot spring or are unwilling to go the few extra miles.
George's 2 cents: This tub was supposedly made by shepherds, hence, Shepherd's Hot Spring. This is a good spot if you want more seclusion and a little hotter water. Water may get too hot in the summer when the sun heats the water in the pond which feeds the spring. To cool tub, move pipe away from tub and let water cool. Nice place to camp too.

The Pond Hot Spring

Location: 1/3 mile southeast of Shepherd's hot spring.
Directions: From Shepherd's Hot Spring, walk or drive a half mile south on a dirt road. Look to your left, to the east. You'll see a pond down the hill in a valley. In the morning or in the evening you may see whisps coming from the pond. The hot spring pond is located at the western edge of the pond. The hot spring is likely the source for the pond.
Seclusion: If you don't mind walking through some slushy grass-lands, you can have this place to yourself.
Fee: Are you kidding?
Temperature: About 90 degrees farenheit.
Camping: There's plenty of free camping nearby.
George's 2 cents: Well, when I visited this place in the spring, it was mucky getting out to it. Water is shallow, about knee deep. If you're really hard-up for a hot spring, this could be fun.

Benton Hot Spring

An extraordinary flow of hot water fills a pond at Benton Hot Springs north of Bishop.

Location: 4 miles west of Benton, California, about 35 miles north of Bishop.

Directions: From Bishop, take Highway 6, 30 miles to Benton. At Benton, take Highway 120, 4 miles west to Benton Hot Springs. You can also reach Benton Hot Springs from Mammoth Lakes by taking Owens River Road to Benton Crossing and following the paved road until it turns into a graded dirt road. Follow this road for about 23.6 miles to Highway 120. Then go east, or turn right, 4 miles to Benton Hot Springs.

Seclusion: There are houses nearby.

Fee: No. However, the hot spring pond is on private land. You should ask permission at the general store before bathing.

Temperature: The source flowing into the pond is 134 degrees farenheit. **Dangerous.**

Condition: This is a natural pond fed by a hot stream of water. The water is too hot and unsafe where the water flows out of a large pipe into the pond. The floor of the pond is mucky. You'll sink about one foot into goo.

Camping: No.

George's 2 cents: Well, let's put it this way: the water is hot in the pond and if you like goo you'll have a good time. It's a shame this hot spring has not been developed. Extraordinarily good flow of hot water being wasted. Benton Hot Springs, or Old Benton, was originally a silver mining town in the 1860's. It's a nice quiet place to visit. Hot in the summer though. Spring and fall are nice.

Mammoth Lakes Hot Springs

Red's Meadow Hot Spring

Location: Near Red's Meadow camp ground at Mammoth Lakes.

Directions: In Mammoth, take California 203 to the ski lifts on Mammoth Mountain. Road continues down a winding paved road to Red's Meadow.

Seclusion: There are six private rooms.

Fee: None for hot spring.

Temperature: Flows out of the ground at 110 degrees farenheit.

Condition: Clean cement tubs.

Camping: Yes, at nearby Red's Meadow campground.

George's 2 cents: The hot spring source is closed to visitor's during the summer season, Memorial Day to Labor Day. The hot water is used during this time to heat the showers and the six private bath tubs in the campground. Baths are available on a first come, first served basis. A metal grate covers the hot spring during summer. When the summer season is over, the metal grate is taken off and the hot spring is used by locals and cross country skiers or hikers.

Fish Creek Hot Spring

Location: 12 miles south of Red's Meadow campground.

Directions: From Red's Meadow campground, hike south on the Fish Creek Trail beyond Island Crossing in Fish Valley. Just past Sharktooth Creek Trail, cross the creek to Iva Bell Camp. The hot

44

spring is about 100 yards up a path which passes through the campground. There are three pools.

Seclusion: Good.

Fee: None.

Temperature: About 110 degrees farenheit.

Condition: Primitive but nice after a long hike.

Camping: Yes, nearby.

George's 2 cents: Being by nature lazy, I did not hike 12 miles to check this hot spring. However, I did interview a person who has visited the hot spring several times. The directions come from him. So if they're wrong, I'll give you his name so you can shoot him or something.

Fish Creek Hot Spring is a fine place to relax after a long hike. The only thing wrong with this place is that you can't drive to it. So I'm not an environmental nut. OK, I'm lying. I'm glad there isn't a road to this place. Have fun when you find it and send me a black and white picture. I need one for the revised edition of this book.

Mono Lake Hot Springs

There are hot springs on the south, west and north shores of Mono Lake. We will begin with the south shore.

Navy Beach Hot Spring

Location: 11 miles southeast of Lee Vining.

Directions: From Lee Vining, take Highway 395, 5.2 miles south to Highway 120. Take Highway 120 east 4 miles until you reach a road sign, "Tufa Reserve." Turn left, north, down a dirt road toward Mono Lake. The road forks. Take the Navy Beach road. It goes to the right. You'll come to another dirt road that goes east and west. Turn left, and follow the road a half mile to the Navy Beach parking area. Take the path on the west side of the parking lot 1/4 mile to the hot spring.

Seclusion: Best times for privacy are in the early morning and at night. Best seasons for private visits are spring and fall.

Fee: None

Temperature: 95 degrees farenheit.

Condition: Primitive. About the size of a large jacuzzi. There are hidden rocks in the pool. **DO NOT DIVE OR JUMP IN.** By the way, the water contains arsenic. Do not drink it.

Camping: Not permitted.

George's 2 cents: This hot spring is on State property because it is a part of the Mono Lake Tufa Reserve. The head ranger does not want people to know about this hot spring. The reason: large numbers of nude bathers have offended visiting tourists. Last year bathers were not allowed to use the hot spring during the summer. High bacteria count was given as the reason.

Please use discretion. Do not bathe nude in the summer during the day. If you desire to do so, the early morning or evening will be the best times during summer. There's a good chance the hot spring will be closed to use in the summer.

I enjoy visiting Navy Beach, especially around sunset. It's much like visiting the ocean; there is the strong smell of salt in the air. And usually there's a nice breeze off the water.

Stay on the main roads while visiting the Tufa Reserve. Be careful not to get stuck in the pumice sand. Two wheel drive cars and trucks can get stuck easily. Stay on the main road.

I remember one night, a friend and I who were singing at Whisky Creek at Mammoth Lakes, got the bright idea to go to Hawthorne, Nevada to gamble. This was like 2:30 in the morning. So we took off in a little Toyota. Going down Pole Line Road north of Mono Lake, we got another bright idea: Let's stop and look at the stars. So we pulled to the side of the road, right into the pumice sand. We got out and admired the night Sierra sky. Got back in and tried to drive but we couldn't get out.

To make a long story short, we slept in the car that night. The following morning someone with a truck and a tow chain hauled us out.

If you do get stuck in the sand, deflate the tires slightly so that they are broader where they meet the sand. Then ease your way out.

46

The author tries out the Navy Beach hot spring on the southern shore of Mono Lake. Water was great, about 95 degrees farenheit. Do not dive or jump in. Hidden rocks are located beneath the surface. The rangers will appreciate it if you bathe clothed during the summer tourist season.

Warm Springs

Location: On the extreme western shore of Mono Lake.
Directions: A road east of the Tufa Reserve goes out to Warm Springs. It's about 10 miles from the Tufa Reserve to Warm Springs.
Caution: Do not attempt to make it in a two wheel drive truck or car. 4-wheel drive vehicles only. Carry drinking water and tell someone where you are going.
Seclusion: You probably can run stark raving naked out here for months.
Fee: No.
Temperature: Like lukewarm bath water.
Condition: Primitive. The spring is now just a trickle compared to what it was in the past. There is no pool now. However, the springs

at one time were developed. Might be worth developing again.

Camping: You can probably camp here till doomsday, providing you've got enough food and fresh water.

George's 2 cents: OK, let's say you're insane or demonically possessed and wanted some place to live out your madness in peace. Warm Springs could be the place. In other words, only the adventurous and those with 4-wheel drive will go to Warm Springs. It's tricky getting out there in the pumice sand but it will certainly be a lot of fun for the adventurous or stupid. Have a great time and don't say I didn't tell you so.

Warm Springs served as a watering stop for the Bodie and Benton Railroad until 1917. The railroad carried wood from the forested area southeast of Mono Lake, to Bodie, a booming mining town in the 1880's. Wood was used for fuel and housing. In 1917 the tracks were torn up and hauled away. You may still find railroad ties of the old track.

Dechambeau Ranch Hot Spring:

Location: On the north shore of Mono Lake northeast of Black Point.

Directions: From Lee Vining, take Highway 395, 4.8 miles to the Mono Lake Park and Cemetery Road. Follow the road past the park and the cemetery. It turns into a well graded dirt road. When you cross Mill Creek, that's the first creek, the road forks. Go left and follow it about 4.5 miles. You'll come to a place where the road forks three ways. Take the center road and follow it .6 miles along the fence. You'll come to a small cabin on your right. Park here. Then walk north, that's to your right when you're facing the ponds. You'll come to a fenced concrete tub with hot water pouring into it. **DO NOT USE OR GO NEAR THIS TUB. EXTREMELY HOT WATER. CHILDREN SHOULD BE HELD AND CAUTIONED.** Continue walking north about 200 yards until you come to a pond. Here there is a small primitive pond.

48

A crude pool has been built at the edge of a warm pond at Dechambeau hot spring north of Mono Lake. Water is piped from a deep well to the pond.

Accessibility: May be impossible to reach in winter even with 4-wheel drive.

Seclusion: Yes, plenty.

Fee: None.

Temperature: About 105 degrees farenheit at the above mentioned pond.

Condition: Primitive.

Camping: Ask permission of owner.

George's 2 cents: This hot spring is on private property. It's always best to ask the owner if you may use the hot spring. There was no one around when I visited the place.

Two wheel drive vehicles should stay on the main road and not go into the pumice sand.

Here's the story on this place: some time ago they were drilling for oil out here. They didn't hit oil but extremely hot water. Keep in mind: this is a volcanic area. Anyway, they piped the water north to a concrete tub that was supposedly used to scald pigs.

Paoha Island Hot Springs
Location: In Hot Springs Cove on Paoha Island in the middle of Mono Lake.
Directions: Get a boat and head out to Paoha Island, the larger island.
Seclusion: More seclusion than any normal human being could want.
Fee: You gotta be kidding.
Temperature: The source is something like 180 degrees farenheit. **Extraordinarily dangerous.**
Condition: Primitive to say the least.
Camping: Sure, you can camp on the island, but not during the nesting season.
George's 2 cents: The islands are off limits during the summer when the seagulls are nesting. I'll be honest with you, I have not visited the Island or the hot springs. But I've heard stories about men boiling eggs in them. Whether or not there is a place where the hot springs meet with cold Mono Lake water where it might be comfortable to bathe, I am not certain. If you do attempt to reach Paoha Island, be certain to wear a life jacket. Even if the day is clear and the water is placid, Mono Lake can turn into a raging ocean without notice. Several people lost their lives on the lake not long ago. Be careful and be safe. Let someone know where you are going and when you intend to return. Bring plenty of fresh water and food. There are no convenience stores on Paoha Island.

Bridgeport Hot Springs

The Hot Springs(Big Hot)

Location: 1.1 mile south of Bridgeport, California.
Directions: 1.1 miles south of Bridgeport, a dirt road off Highway 395 leads east to the hot springs. There are six pools, but the largest, called "Big Hot," is the most often used. If approaching from the south, turn right onto the dirt road. You will come to a gate. Open it, drive through and go back and shut it. The gate keeps grazing cattle where they belong instead of playing "dodge the cars " out on 395. Follow the dirt road for about 1/2 mile. This road has lots of deep ruts.

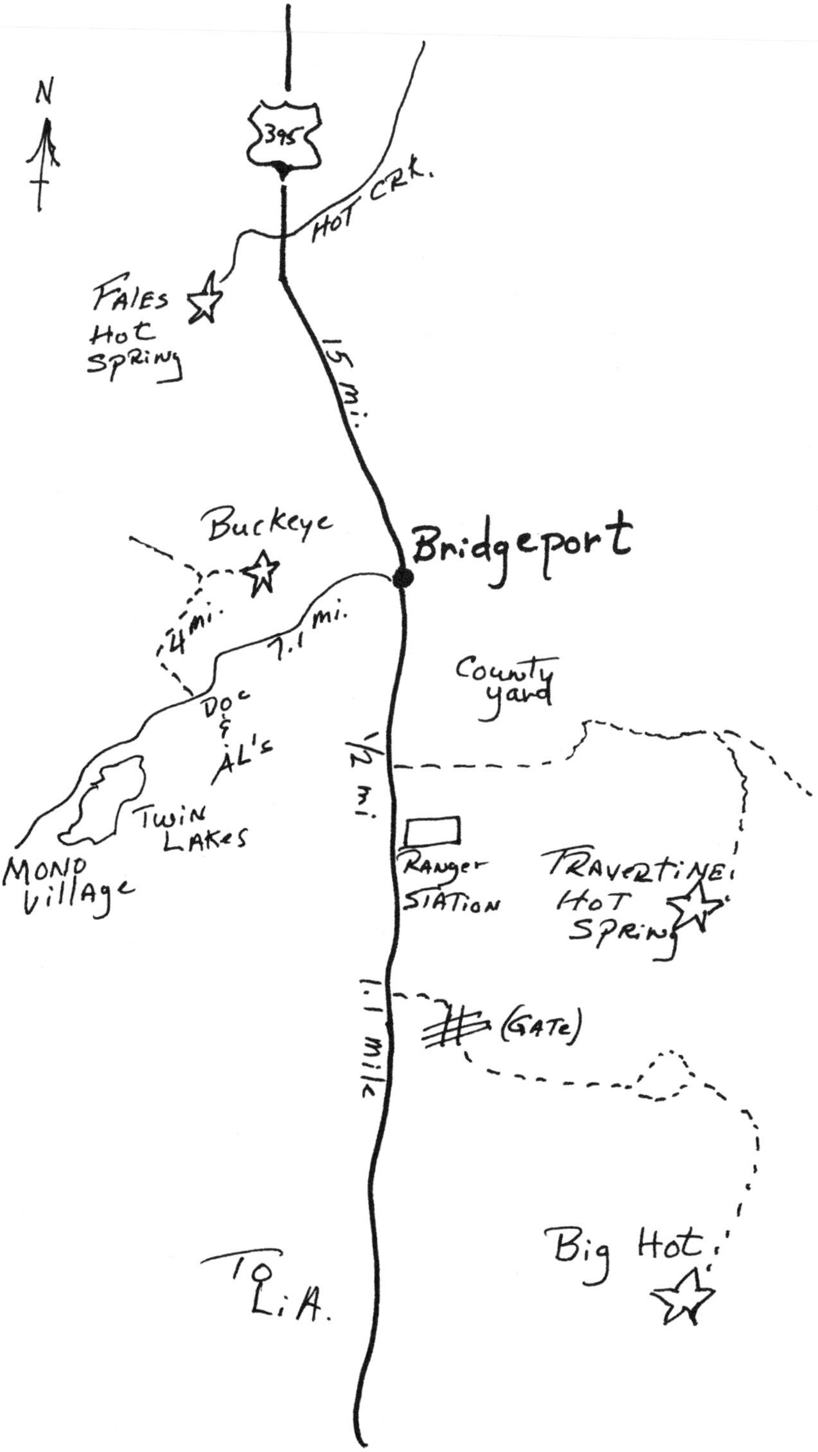

N

395

HOT CRK.

FALES
Hot
Spring

15 mi.

Buckeye

Bridgeport

County
yard

4 mi.

7.1 mi.

Doc
&
AL's

½ mi.

TWIN
LAKES

Ranger
STATION

TRAVERTINE
HOT
SPRING

MONO
Village

1.1 mile

(GATE)

TO
L.A.

Big Hot.

would not suggest RV's or large trailers trying to make it in. You will shortly come to a white chalk hill. Two steep roads in poor condition go up the hill. If you're in a vehicle that can't make the grade, you can park here. Walk or drive up the hill and follow the road. You'll come to the hot spring pools about a 1/4 mile away.

Accessibility: You will need 4-wheel drive in winter.

Seclusion: Depending on the time of day, you can have the hot springs to yourselves. I would suggest mornings before 10, evenings around 5.

Fee: None.

Temperature: Warm but not hot. Like regular bath water.

Condition: This is a natural hot springs pool and it's deep. Young children should wear life jackets. There is a rock ledge around the sides.

Camping: Yes.

George's 2 cents: This is one of my very favorite hot springs for several reasons. It's easy to reach from the highway. Often you can have the place to yourself and you can camp nearby. It is also an historic spot. For centuries the Paiute Indians camped, bathed and lived beside this pool. If you look around, you may be able to find arrowheads. A friend of mine collected scores of arrowheads in this area. It's a nice place. Please keep it clean and safe. In the spring around April, be careful not to get stuck in the mud. I got stuck once and had to be hauled out.

Travertine Hot Spring

Location: 1 mile southeast of Bridgeport.

Directions: Go south from Bridgeport .5 miles; a road goes to the east toward the County buildings. Turn left and follow the road 1/4 mile. Then turn left on a dirt road and follow it 1.3 miles up, then down, then up a hill. Portions of this road are quite rutted. I made it in with my trailer but I had to be careful. You will come up a hill and there will be a long ridge of travertine, rock, on your right. Turn right here and follow the road on the east side of the rock ridge.

A large pool of warm green water makes for an enjoyable afternoon at Big Hot near Bridgeport. The hot spring was a popular place for the Paiute Indians. Here they camped and collected pine nuts in the nearby hills. You might find an arrowhead if you're lucky.

Accessibility: You will need 4-wheel drive in winter.
Seclusion: This is a popular hot spring. Best times for bathing alone will be early in the morning or late at night. Even then you may have company.
Fee: None
Temperature: 95-105 degrees.
Condition: Primitive man made tubs with clay bottoms. Very enjoyable.
Camping: Yes.
George's 2 cents: This is a nicely developed hot spring. And quite interesting too. A spring emerges at the crest of a ridge of travertine. A cut along the ridge carries the water to four hot spring pools located below. One, is large enough for one person and is very hot. Two are about the size of jacuzzi and the water is around 95. The third is a smaller pool and cooler.

Travertine hot spring near Bridgeport. A hot stream of water emerges at the crest of a ridge of travertine. A cut was made along the top of the ridge to carry the water to four pools located below. Temperature ranges from 90-105 degrees farenheit.

This is a popular spot. Even tour buses bring people by in the summer. I like this hot spring very much but if you're looking for privacy, you may be disappointed.

There are several other developed pools in the nearby area. Look around.

Buckeye Hot Spring

Location: About 5 miles west of Bridgeport near Buckeye campground.

Directions: From Bridgeport take Twin Lakes road 7.1 miles to Doc and Al's. Turn right here and follow the dirt road 4 miles toward Buckeye Campground. Just past a one lane bridge, the road forks. Take the second dirt road on your right and follow it up the hill .4

A closer look at the unusual Travertine hot spring source. Hot water emerges farther up this cut and is carried to the pools below.

mile. You'll find a parking area on your right. Park here. You have to walk down a steep trail to the hot spring.

Seclusion: It's visited often in the spring and summer.

Accessibility: You'll need 4-wheel drive in winter and even then it may be impossible.

Fee: None for the hot spring.

Temperature: About 105 degrees farenheit. Temperature can be controlled by a pipe that brings cold water in from the river.

Condition: This is a nice, clear and clean hot spring pool. A rock

Another hot pool at Travertine. There are several separate pools. More are being developed now. Look around the area and see what you can find.

dam holds the water to make a pool.

Camping: Not at the hot spring but at the campground.

George's 2 cents: It appears to be one of the more popular hot springs, especially among those who prefer bathing nude. More private in mornings. If you're looking for privacy, this is not the spot.

Fales Hot Spring

Location: 13 miles north of Bridgeport on Highway 395.

Directions: Take Highway 395, 13 miles north. Fales Hot Springs is on the left side, west side, of the road. There are a group of cabins and an abandoned gas station.

Seclusion: Less visited than other hot springs.

Fee: None at the moment.

Temperature: The source is extraordinarily hot and will burn the hell out of any normal human being.

Buckeye hot spring near Buckeye campground west of Bridgeport. The hot spring is located on the side of a steep hillside. The hot water drains to the edge of a stream where a rock dam has been built. Temperature of the the hot pool is controlled by regulating the incoming cold water from the stream.

Condition: Well, here's the story. The resort is currently closed. Fales was originally a resort started by Sam Fales back in the 1800's. The resort has fallen into disuse the past ten years or so. There is a large concrete pool that is no longer being used. The source itself is on private property. You should ask permission for any use. However, the hot water leads down a creek to the north. I suggest you go about 1/4 mile past Fales and park. Then walk west to the creek. Look for the Southern Pacific box car on the hilltop. Just below this is a large pool. The water is about 105 degrees farenheit. This is also on private property. You should ask for permission from the owner to use the pool.

You may also follow the creek to where it passes underneath the highway and down the east side.

Camping: No, but nearby there is plenty of public land.

George's 2 cents: Fales Hot Spring is currently for sale. I would be

Fales Hot Spring 13 miles north of Bridgeport. The resort is currently for sale. The stone building dates from the early 1880's and was built by Sam Fales.

A waste deep hot pool is located down the creek from Fales.

certain to ask permission of anyone at the property before using the hot spring.

Grover Hot Springs State Park

Location: 4 miles west of Markleeville, California.
Directions: South of Topaz Lake on 395, Highway 89 leads 22 miles over Monitor Pass to Markleeville. The road is steep and curvy. I would not suggest trailers or RV's going up this way. I towed my trailer up and down this road once and I swore I'd never do it again. You can also reach Markleeville from Minden, Nevada by taking Highway 88 south. Markleeville is 22 miles from Minden. Road signs at Markleeville point the way to Grover Hot Springs State Park.
Pool Hours: 9 Am to 9 PM daily.
Seclusion: This is a public place.
Fee: Children $2; adults $3.
Temperature: Two pools; one at 70-80 degrees farenheit, the other at 102-105.
Condition: Good. This is a public resort. There's a campground with outdoor pools, showers and restrooms.
Camping: Yes but there's a fee.
George's 2 cents: Grover's is highly visited during the summer. If you like being around people, you'll like Grover's. There are lots of hiking trails nearby and streams to fish trout. It's a nice place for the family. If you intend to camp, I suggest you make a reservation in advance. Phone (916) 694-2248. By the way, the pools are on a first come, first served basis. The capacity is 50 and this number is reached early during summer days.

Grover Hot Springs on a cold spring afternoon makes an eerie sight. There are two hot pools filled with water from springs which emerge from the hillside above. Camping is available nearby.

Western Nevada Hot Springs

Walley's Hot Spring

Location: In Carson Valley, Nevada just south of Genoa. 15 miles from Lake Tahoe and near Carson City.

Directions: Take Highway 395 north to Minden, Nevada. Just north of Minden, Highway 19 leads west toward the Sierra. When you come to Highway 206, turn right and go about 1 mile to Walley's Hot Springs. Walley's is about 4 miles from Highway 395.

Phone: (702) 782-8155

Pools open: 7 days a week. Hours 8 AM to 10 PM. Friday and Saturday, 8 AM to 11 PM.

Restaurant: Closed Monday and Tuesday.

Address: Box 26, Genoa, Nevada 89411.

Fee: You can become a member or pay a small fee with each visit.

Walley's Hot Spring is a plush resort at the foot of the Sierra Nevada near Lake Tahoe. Lodging, restaurant, bar and weight training room are available.

Temperature: Varies in the six pools.

Condition: This is a top of the line hot spring resort. Absolutely beautiful. Includes a weight training room, sauna, steam bath, massage, lodging rooms, deluxe restaurant, bar, and lovely patio.

Camping: No, but there are hotel rooms on the premises.

George's 2 cents: Walley's Hot Spring is located in one of the most beautiful valleys in the world. The hot spring was developed in the early 1860's. Mark Twain and President Grant are said to have been visitors. At over 4,000 feet, the sun is bright and the sky is generally clear. Walley's is a nice romantic place to get away with the one you love. It's close to Lake Tahoe if you want to gamble or visit the Lake. The bar is cozy. I've enjoyed having a drink, soaking up the bright Nevada sunshine, talking with a friend and taking a dip in the various pools. I think you'll like Walley's.

A large swimming pool and private bathing rooms are available at Carson Hot Springs in Carson City.

Carson City Hot Spring

Location: On Hot Springs Road in Carson City, Nevada
Directions: Coming into Carson City on Highway 395, go to the north end of town. Look for a sign, "Hot Springs Road." Turn right and go until you reach the hot spring resort on your left. It's about a mile.
Phone: (702) 882-9863
Hours: 8 AM-11 PM daily.
Seclusion: This is a public resort. However, you can rent your own private spa room.
Fee: Yes. Pool and patio are $5 adults; $2.50 for seniors and children. Special dis count for frequent visitors: $37.50 for 10 visits. Private rooms are $8 for one person and $14 for two persons.
Temperature: Swimming pool is kept at 98 degrees farenheit in summer, 102 in winter. Private rooms can be controlled at 95-110 degrees farenheit.

Bower's Mansion pool is open from Memorial Day to Labor Day.

Condition: Good. There are nine private cement pools large enough for eight people. There's also a largepublic pool. Towels provided.

Camping: No.

George's 2 cents: Carson Hot Springs is easy to reach and it's a pleasant way to end a long drive. You can bathe in private spas or in the public pool. Camping is not allowed but there is a nearby RV park on Highway 395 about a 1 1/2 miles away. Plus there are nearby grocery stores. Lots of motels if you need a room.

Bower's Mansion:

Location: 10 miles north of Carson City on Highway 395.

Directions: Stay on 395 past Carson. A road sign will be on your right. Look for the mansion on your left, to the west.

Phone: (702) 849-1825.

Open: From Memorial Day to Labor Day.

Seclusion: This is a public swimming pool.

Historic Bower's Mansion in Washoe Valley north of Carson City, was built in the 1860's by Sandy and Eilley Bowers who made millions in the Comstock silver mines. Mansion is open for tours during the summer.

Fee: Yes, but reasonable.

Temperature: About 80 degrees farenheit.

Condition: Large modern swimming pool and wading pool for children.

Camping: Yes, nearby but not at pool.

George's 2 cents: Bowers' Mansion is a nice place to spend Sunday afternoon with the family. There are green lawns for picnics, barbecue grills and you can visit the historic Bower's Mansion. Originally built and owned by Sandy and Eilley Bowers, who made millions in the Comstock silver mines, today the mansion is a popular tourist attraction. Small entrance fee.

There is camping nearby at Davis Creek Campground north about 1 mile.

Steamboat Hot Spring near Reno is currently being restored and is due to be open in late 1987.

Steamboat Hot Spring

Location: 11 miles south of Reno on the east side of Highway 395.
Directions: Just stay on 395 past Carson City about 19 miles. You'll seea white California mission styled building on the east side of the highway.
Seclusion: Both private and public bathing.
Fee: Unknown.
Temperature: Varies with pools.
Condition: Resort is currently being renovated.
Camping: No.
George's 2 cents: Well, here's the story: The resort was recently taken over by a church who is renovating it. Part of the resort will be open to the public toward the end of 1987.

Historical note: Steamboat Hot Spring has been a resort since the 1860's. Miners and others from nearby Virginia City appreciated the resort's soothing waters. Mark Twain was a visitor to Steamboat Hot Springs in 1863 while he was a reporter for the *Territorial Enterprise* at Virginia City.

Gerlach Hot Springs

Location: 3/4 mile northwest of Gerlach, Nevada.

Directions: From Reno, take I-80 east to the Wadsworth exit. Then take Highway 447 north to Gerlach. It's 107 miles from Reno to Gerlach. At Gerlach, go 1/2 mile from the old train station on Nevada 447.

Condition: There is a large cement soaking pool recently built and a mud bath. There are changing rooms and restrooms.

Fee: Yes.

Seclusion: This is a public place. Bathing suits are required.

Temperature: About 100 degrees farenheit.

Camping: Yes.

George's 2 cents: The hot springs are currently closed for renovation. I was told the pools may be open in 1988. Sorry but there is no phone number at the hot springs to check this one out.

The source of hot water for Steamboat Hot Spring resort near Reno.

About the Author

George Williams III is the author of ten books. He was recently nominated for the Pulitzer Prize in Letters for his book, **Mark Twain: His Life In Virginia City, Nevada.** He has recently completed a series of four books about Mark Twain's life in California and Nevada 1861-68. His book, **Rosa May: The Search For A Mining Camp Legend,** is planned for a television movie.

George lives with his family in the Sierra Nevada where he is writing additional books about the Eastern Sierra.

George is available for talks and seminars. If you would like him to speak to your group, please write him in care of the publisher.

Order these GREAT books by mail today! Each <u>autographed</u> and <u>personally inscribed</u> to you by George Williams III!

ROSA MAY: THE SEARCH FOR A MINING CAMP LEGEND Virginia City, Carson City and Bodie California were towns Rosa May worked as a prostitute and madam between 1873-1912. Read her remarkable true story based on 3 1/2 years of intensive research. Includes 30 rare photos and 26 personal letters of Rosa May's recently discovered. 240 pages. **AUTOGRAPHED BY THE AUTHOR.** Soft cover quality, $9.95; hard cover, gold embossed, $18.95. Soon to be a television movie.
"Both stories—Rosa May's and the author's—are told in a rich, deeply personal and yet scholarly work of regional history."
Los Angeles Times Book Review.

THE GUIDE TO BODIE AND EASTERN SIERA HISTORIC SITES True story of the rise and fall of Bodie—California's most famous gold mining town, today a ghost town, California State Park and National Historic Site. Once known as the most violent mining town in the West, murders were a daily occurrence in this mountain town where millions were made in a few years. A beautiful full color cover with over 100 rare, historic photos. 88 pages. Quality soft cover, $9.95; hard cover, gold embossed, $18.95.
"A fine account of the rise and fall of Bodie—one of the West's most famous gold mining towns."
Pasadena Star News

THE MURDERS AT CONVICT LAKE True story of the infamous 1871 Nevada State Penitentiary break in which 29 outlaws—murderers, rapists, train robbers—escaped. Six convicts fled more than 200 miles into Mono and Inyo counties California in the Eastern Sierra. They pledged to kill anyone who got in their way. Near Bridgeport they killed a young Pony Express rider, Billy Poor. In a terrible shootout at Monte Diablo, today known as Convict lake near Mammoth Lakes ski resort, the convicts killed two men. They fled south to Bishop where they were captured, tried and two convicts hanged. Here is the intense true story based on newspaper accounts of the day and public records. 18 rare, historic photos and dramatic scene depictions by Dave Comstock, well known artist and author. **AUTOGRAPHED BY THE AUTHOR.** Quality soft cover, $4.95; hard cover, gold embossed, $12.95.

"...rich in both text and pictures. As always, Williams captures the flavor of his subject in great detail, while capturing the reader's interest...a must for anyone wishing to know more about our rich history."
Buddy Noonan, The Review, Mammoth Lakes

THE REDLIGHT LADIES OF VIRGINIA CITY, NEVADA

Virginia City, Nevada near Reno was the richest mining camp in the American West. The silver from its mines built San Francisco and helped the Union win the Civil War. The town prospered from 1860-1895. The town had one of the largest redlight districts in America. Virginia City's wealth attracted women from all parts of the world. Author Williams tells of the strange lives of the redlight girls, of their legends and violent deaths. Here is the true story of madam Jessie Lester, shot by her lover yet refused to give police his name. And Julia Bulette, the highly respected prostitute who was violently murdered in her bed. Based on newspaper accounts, county records and U.S. Census materials. Perhaps the most informative book on American prostitution in the old West. Many rare, historic photos of prostitutes, madams, pimps. Includes historic letters by prostitutes, madams, lovers and other historic documents. **AUTOGRAPHED BY THE AUTHOR.** Quality soft cover, $5.95; hard cover, gold embossed $12.95.

"Rare photos, maps and letters from prostitutes, madams and lovers spark this treatise on the world's oldest profession as practiced in the richest mining town in the West in the late nineteenth century." **True West**

New Mark Twain in the West Series!
Critically acclaimed by Mark Twain historians and fans.
Based on recently disocvered letters and journals, four new books reveal intimate details of Mark Twain's life in California and Nevada.

MARK TWAIN: HIS ADVENTURES AT AURORA AND MONO LAKE When Sam Clemens arrived in Nevada, August, 1861, he hoped to strike it rich in the silver mines. For six months he tried prospecting and silver mining at Aurora, Nevada, near Bodie, California. Clemens didn't strike it rich but his hard luck mining days led to his writing career. Based on Mark Twain's own letters, this book gives readers a firsthand account of Clemens' life as a struggling miner. Points out places, like Mono Lake, where Mark Twain camped, fished and hiked, places you can visit today. Over 60 rare, historic photos, some published here for the first time. 100 pages. **AUTOGRAPHED BY THE AUTHOR.** Quality soft cover, $6.95; hard cover, gold embossed, $12.95.
"Williams has thoroughly covered an important aspect of Mark Twain's life as a silver miner."
Bill Dalton, Historian and Publisher

MARK TWAIN: HIS LIFE IN VIRGINIA CITY, NEVADA
Having failed to strike it rich at Aurora and gone broke, Clemens is offered a reporting job by the *Territorial Enterprise* in Virginia City. At first reluctant to give up his mining endeavors, Clemens relents and takes the job. He walks more than 130 miles to Virginia City across the Nevada desert. Arriving in mid-October, 1862 Clemens begins a twenty-one month stint as local reporter, a job which permanently changed his life. Here Clemens adopted Mark Twain as his pen name and won notoriety as a humorist and character. Williams shows us the young Mark Twain was a fun loving hell raiser who drank too much, invented horrible murder stories and fled town after threatening a rival editor to duel. Williams also gives the true account of how Clemens really got his name, "Mark Twain." Re-

vealed for the first time in this account. **AUTOGRAPHED BY THE AUTHOR.** 208 pages. 60 rare, historical photographs. Quality soft cover, $9.95; hard cover, gold embossed, $24.95.

"...provides much information about the Territorial Enterprise, and Twain's associates on the paper..One useful section provides current maps and instructions for visiting the sites of Twain's days in Nevada."
Kirkus Reviews

NEW FOR 1988! **MARK TWAIN: JACKASS HILL AND THE JUMPING FROG** In May, 1864, Mark Twain leaves Virginia City for San Francisco. At first Twain reports for the San Francisco *Call*. Finding the *Call's* editor and the work repressive, Twain begins his associations with Bret Harte and other well known West Coast writers. Twain begins a successful career as a free lance writer contributing to the *Golden Era* and the *Californian*. After a dispute with police, Twain fleas town for Jim Gillis' Jackass Hill cabin near Sonora. Here Twain stays for three months, learns about pocket gold mining and discovers the "Jumping Frog of Calaveras County, " story. The story, published in 1865, creates instant national success for Twain. Many rare, historic photos. **AUTOGRAPHED BY THE AUTHOR.** Quality soft cover, $5.95; hard cover, gold embossed, $12.95.

"Williams for the first time shows how important Mark Twain's three month stay on Jackass Hill was to his first literary success. Much funny and useful information here."
Riverside Press-Enterprise

NEW FOR 1988! **ON THE ROAD WITH MARK TWAIN IN CALIFORNIA AND NEVADA** Here is a wonderful travel guide to places where Mark Twain lived, wrote, mined and camped while living in California and Nevada, 1861-68. Williams tells what Twain was doing at each historic site. This is a book for the traveler who wishes to visit Twain's historic haunts and is looking for general information about Twain's life in California and Nevada. Includes useful road maps and road directions to all historic sites. Many historic photographs and photos of historic sites as they look today. **AUTOGRAPHED BY THE AUTHOR.** Quality soft cover, $9.95; hard cover, gold embossed, $18.95.

"When it comes to writing useful travel guides, Williams is a champ. This useful book is intersting and plain fun. Every Twain fan should have this book."

Bill Dalton, Historian and Publisher

New For 1988! HOT SPRINGS OF THE EASTERN SIERRA 40 major hot springs in the Eastern Sierra, road directions, maps. 72 pages 5.95 pap, 12.95 hard cover. **AUTOGRAPHED BY THE AUTHOR.**

Use Visa or MasterCard to order by phone by calling <u>toll FREE</u> 1-800-346-8221. Outside California call (619) 932-7590.

ORDER FORM

Name_____Address_____

City_____State_____Zip_____

Please send me the following:

___Copy(ies) ROSA MAY ___pap. $9.95 ___hard cover 18.95

___Copy (ies) GUIDE TO BODIE___pap. 9.95___hard cover $18.95

___Copy(ies) MURDERS AT CONVICT LAKE___pap 4.95___hard cover 12.95

___Copy(ies) REDLIGHT LADIES OF VIRGINIA CITY ___pap 5.95___hard cover 12.95

___Copy(ies) MARK TWAIN; HIS ADVENTURES AT AURORA ___pap 6.95
        ___hard cover 12.95

----Copy(ies) MARK TWAIN: HIS LIFE IN VIRGINIA CITY___pap 9.95
        ___hard cover 24.95

___Copy(ies) MARK TWAIN: JACKASS HILL AND THE JUMPING FROG
        ___pap 5.95___hard cover 12.95

___Copy(ies) ON THE ROAD WITH MARK TWAIN IN CALIFORNIA AND NEVADA
        ___pap 9.95 ___hard cover $18.95

___Copy(ies) HOT SPRINGS OF THE EASTERN SIERRA ___pap 5.95 ___Hard cover
        12.95

Total for books $_____

Add $1.50 postage for 1st book, .50 each additional book.

Total Enclosed $_____

Send checks or money orders to:

Mail to: Tree By The River Publishing, Box 463-HS, Bridgeport, CA 93517

Thank you for your mail order!!!